Bear Dogs

CANINES WITH A MISSION

TED WOOD

Walker & Company
New York

INTRODUCTION

LATE ONE SUMMER DAY a phone call comes from Glacier National Park, Montana. "We have black bears along our park road," the ranger says to biologist Carrie Hunt, "and we can't control them. We need help from you and your team."

Like wildlife superheroes, Carrie and her human partners—Tim, Brian, and Angie—spring into action. They pile their team of six excited dogs into the back of two trucks and speed off to the park, three hours from their base in Whitefish, Montana. The bear busters are on the job again.

Every year more and more bears get into trouble as they lose their natural fear of humans. Attracted by our tasty food, they break into houses and raid campgrounds, trash cans, and even cars. In the end, the bears pay for their boldness with their lives. Carrie's sole mission is to teach people and bears to live together peacefully, so that bears will always have a place in the forest and in our hearts.

But how do you teach a bear to be a good bear? Carrie thinks she has the answer in her four-legged instructors—Karelian bear dogs. These black and white husky-like dogs come from a region of Finland called Karelia, where they have been used for 400 years to hunt brown bears. Finnish legends tell of brave bear dogs that have saved their masters from bears, sometimes leaping on the backs of angry bruins. They are fearless and so fast that they can jump out of the way of a swiping paw.

However, Carrie doesn't want to hunt bears, she wants to save them. When she heard about the big-hearted Karelians in 1990, she saw a new way to scare bears away from the places where humans live and play. By barking at and chasing wayward bears, the dogs can teach them to stay where they best belong—away from human contact.

In 1995 Carrie started the Wind River Bear Institute and the Partners in Life program, using Karelian bear dogs to tackle bear emergencies throughout the West. This is the story of Carrie's brave dog team led by Cassie, the first Karelian canine in the world to teach young dogs and old bears new tricks.

"NO EGGS FOR YOU this morning, Tuffy," Carrie says to the hovering bear dog behind her. It's dawn, and Carrie and Angie are shoveling down their breakfasts before going on patrol.

The team arrived late the night before at a small trailer Carrie moved to the Many Glacier campground that summer, home to operation bear scare in Glacier National Park. Today they will look for black bears eating plants and flowers along the main road into Many Glacier. These roadside bears are no longer scared of the crowds of tourists who stop to watch them, and the park is worried about the safety of both.

"Load up!" Carrie commands her team. Rio and Cassie fly into Carrie's truck sensing action, and Tess, Tuffy, Yoki, and Eilu jump into Tim's camper.

The dogs can smell a bear before anyone can see it. Five minutes from the campground, they go off like firecrackers, barking and bouncing around the camper. Carrie rounds a corner and sees a stopped car and its driver casually taking pictures of a mother bear with three cubs walking through the grass. We have to give her a good scare, Carrie thinks, so her cubs learn to stay away from roads too.

Carrie, Brian, Tim, and Angie each grab a barking, excited dog, attaching themselves to leashes to control the dogs' actions. "Bark at the bear!" Carrie commands her team. The dogs break into a frenzy of howls and are pulling so hard the handlers can barely hold them. Carrie gives a signal, and the dogs charge off toward the startled mother and her cubs, dragging their humans behind. "Get out of here, bear!" the handlers shout.

Mother bear is petrified of this crazy group rushing toward her. She dashes back into the trees and pushes her cubs up a tall pine, climbing up behind them. The team reaches the tree and the dogs go berserk. Seeing his first bear ever, the youngest dog, Yoki, tries to climb the tree, leaping like a rabbit while the others bark and the humans scream. It's a noisy, scary scene for all the bears watching from high up in the pine.

"OK, leave it!" Carrie yells out. Instantly the dogs stop barking. Mother bear is now in a good bear place, away from the road and humans. Carrie hopes she's learned a lesson about where she can and can't be.

But the lesson is only half over. By now there's a huge bear traffic jam on the road. Everyone hopes to see the hiding bears again. But just as much, they hope to meet the brave dogs they saw chasing the bears away. As people gather around, Carrie explains how she saves bears by scaring them. She tells the crowd that if they want to help too, they shouldn't stop to watch the roadside bears. Once a bear gets used to humans, it will venture into other human areas looking for food. Then, if it develops a taste for human food, it's very hard, even for Carrie's team, to teach it to stay away. Many bears end up having to be destroyed, and nobody wants that. Even as she talks, the bear dogs watch the tree line intensely, barking a warning now and then.

Back at the campground, it's time for everyone to relax. Never forgetting her four-legged teammates, Carrie doles out doggie snacks. Just before bedtime, the dogs have their campground walk. Like royal ambassadors for Partners in Life, they strut from campsite to campsite, greeting the campers. Though fierce around bears, Karelian bear dogs love people and are quick to give out friendly licks.

After the dogs are settled, Tim enters the trailer with some urgent news. Along with being a bear dog handler, Tim is a Montana State bear biologist. Over his radio he heard of big bear trouble in the small town of Polebridge, four hours away. Grizzlies there are breaking into people's homes and wandering through town looking for food. Fearing the situation is desperate, Tim and Carrie decide to leave for Polebridge in the morning.

Tiny Polebridge sits against the west side of Glacier National Park and is so small there is only one store in town. People around the area have lived peacefully with bears for a long time, but now eight grizzlies have started raiding some of the new homes, attracted to improperly stored food.

The problem is getting out of control, fast. Carrie fears that if they can't stop the rampage, the bears will have to be destroyed. The team first heads for a house where the worst break-in happened the day before. That morning, instead of finding her dogs peacefully asleep on her porch, the owner was shocked to discover a huge mother grizzly with two cubs napping on the dogs' couch. The bear family had walked in through the open porch door the night before, and the dogs had fled in terror. The bears had then eaten a 50-pound bag of dog food and were so full they fell right to sleep.

When the Karelian dog team arrives the grizzly family is gone. Just to be sure, Carrie hooks up Cassie and turns on her radio tracker, which picks up signals from radio-collared bears. Bear smell is everywhere but Cassie picks up the freshest trail and leads Carrie to the edge of the forest. Carrie suspects the culprit is Star, the mother bear. Star has been in trouble often, and Carrie has tracked her before. She's very clever and hard to catch. Park rangers have put a radio collar on Star to help them keep track of her.

Carrie tunes her receiver to Star's collar frequency and listens for a signal. Slowly changing the direction of her antenna, she hears it—a strong clicking sound not far off in the trees. Star and her cubs are waiting out there. Believing that the bears will return for more food, Carrie and her team set a trap. They hide in the garage and a small shed, one on each side of the house, ready to surprise the bears with barking dogs and harmless but stinging rubber bullets from Tim's shotgun.

17

After hours of waiting, Carrie realizes something's not right. She knows by the unchanging radio signals that the bears haven't moved. Then a voice comes over Tim's radio. Bears have been spotted at an empty house breaking into a shed. To everyone's surprise, the house is close by, but hidden in the forest. That's why the radio signals stayed the same.

The team jumps into their trucks and roars off to the scene of the break-in. They circle the area and pull into the long dirt driveway. Suddenly, another grizzly appears on the road on his way to the house. It's Louie, a teenage male also with a bad record. Cassie and Tess charge after Louie barking. Carrie is yelling "Get out of here, bear!" and Tim fires harmless exploding shells, like firecrackers, over Louie's head. The scene is enough to frighten even the biggest bear, and Louie turns and disappears into the safety of the forest.

"Good job on the bear!" Carrie says to Cassie and Tess, giving them their snack rewards. They continue down the driveway to the house and spot Star and her cubs running from the shed into the woods. Star had ripped a hole in the flimsy door and gorged herself on horse oats stored in open metal barrels. Carrie knows just how dangerous this could be for the bear and her family. Without meaning to, the homeowner has lured Star to break into his house. That kind of bad behavior may get her killed. And if she dies, her cubs might die too.

Carrie and Tim decide to set another trap for Star. This time it's a metal tube-shaped trap with a sliding door that will capture Star and her cubs, and give the team a chance to teach Star a lesson she'll never forget. Tim puts the trap next to the shed and baits it with deer meat he's been carrying for just this purpose. The team then leaves for the night.

Early the next morning the bear busters return to the house. Right away, Carrie notices the closed trap door. Star is finally caught. But when she peeks in the metal door she sees it's not Star at all. It's Louie! And he looks just like a kid who got caught stealing candy. Louie's in for a good scolding from the team, but first Tim and Carrie want to examine him.

Tim tranquilizes Louie with a shot attached to the end of a long stick and waits for him to fall asleep. Then the team pulls him from the trap and covers his open eyes with a cloth to protect them from injury. They weigh and measure him, take his temperature, and check the condition of his teeth and claws. Tess also examines the sleeping bear before the team wraps a new radio collar around his neck and puts him back into the trap.

Late in the afternoon, Louie is awake and ready to go, but not without his lesson. Tim positions the trap facing the forest. Then he and his assistant grab their shotguns and climb to the top of the camper. Carrie and her crew stand nearby with the dogs leashed and ready to go. With a long cable, Tim's assistant opens the trap door. Louie comes flying out and the shotguns fire. Rubber bullets and beanbags bounce off Louie's rear end. "Bark at the bear!" Carrie commands her dogs. They too go off like cannons, and as Louie flees in terror into the trees, the bear dogs bound after him, driving home the unpleasant lesson. Just two minutes later, the quiet of the forest returns. The team performed perfectly, and Carrie knows that Louie will think twice about visiting homes again. Many bears only need one good lesson like this to change their bad behavior forever.

BY THE END OF FALL, the bears retreat to their dens for the winter and it is time for Carrie to take her team to their Utah home. During the summer the dogs worked 29 grizzly bears and 39 black bears. As a result of the team's effort, none were destroyed, and even Louie kept his nose clean.

But just as important as teaching bears better habits is teaching people better behavior around bears. So Carrie and Cassie have a bear-and-dog show they take to schools everywhere. First Cassie sits up and gives Carrie a high-five hello. Then Cassie becomes a bear gone bad, begging for food from tourists.

"What happens to a bear who begs for food?" Carrie asks. Cassie answers by rolling over on her back with her legs in the air.

"That's right, Cassie. It's shot and killed. So always make sure your campsite is clean and never attract bears with food. It might kill them," Carrie tells the kids.

Back home, the bear dogs watch for Carrie's return from the top of their kennels—all but one, that is. There's a new puppy on the team, and Carrie can't wait to start training little Cassidy. But before he can learn bear tricks, Cassidy must learn to get by in the crazy world of humans. So off they go to Park City, where Cassidy faces hundreds of tourists, cars, other dogs, and kids who want to pull his ears and kiss him. Like Carrie's other Karelians, Cassidy turns out to be a people lover.

Carrie couldn't be prouder of her new team member. With Cassidy lying next to her in bed that night, she's reminded of young Cassie, their beginnings ten years ago, and the hundreds of bears the dogs have saved since. Cassidy will grow into a leader just like Cassie did. Through Partners in Life, he will help save hundreds more bears and teach the world that humans and bears can live peacefully together.

HOW TO KEEP A GOOD BEAR GOOD

Following a few simple rules in bear country, you can help keep a good bear from turning bad. Remember, human food is deadly to bears—the more they eat the closer they come to being destroyed.

In camp:
- Set up your tent 30-50 yards or as far away as possible from your cooking area, so a bear doesn't think your tent is the kitchen.
- Always keep your campsite clean of food and garbage. Wash dishes and pots quickly after meals. Store all food, including utensils, in a bear-proof container like your car, or hang it from a high tree branch.
- Never bury garbage. Bears have great noses and are expert diggers.
- Change clothes after you've eaten dinner and put them in the car. You don't want clothes smelling like food in your tent.
- Never keep food in your tent, including toothpaste, gum, and candy. Bears even like the smell of camera film, so keep that in your car too.
- If your pet is camping with you, store its food just like you store yours.
- Don't leave your camp before all food and trash is properly stored. Even in daylight a bear will raid a camp if it smells food.

On a hike:
- Never approach a bear, especially one with cubs. Bears are sometimes curious, but they are still wild.
- Bears don't like surprises. Let them know you're coming. Hike with friends or family and make enough noise that a bear can hear you and move away. Bears are generally shy but can be dangerous if surprised.
- Don't leave your backpack on the trail and run off to see something. Bears know that packs often carry food.

This book is dedicated to Cassie, the Partners in Life lead dog. Working at Carrie's side from the program's beginning, Cassie helped pioneer bear shepherding, a new technique that offers problem bears an alternative to relocation or destruction. Cassie died at age nine on April 6, 1999, in Carrie's arms. This canine hero changed bear management for all time, and her pups have stepped forward to continue her ground-breaking work.

You may want to discuss with your parents the possibility of contributing part of your allowance to help support these dog heroes. Contact:

The Wind River Bear Institute
PO Box 307
Heber City, UT 84032

E-mail: windriver@shadowlink.net
Web site: www.beardogs.org

First published in the United States of America in 2001 by Walker Publishing Company, Inc.

Published simultaneously in Canada by Fitzhenry and Whiteside, Markham, Ontario L3R 4T8

Title page photograph © Scott Sine

Book design by M. Fadden Rosenthal/mspaceny

Library of Congress Cataloging-in-Publication Data
Wood, Ted, 1965-
   Bear dogs : canines with a mission / Ted Wood.
      p. cm.
   ISBN 0-8027-8758-4 (Hardcover) — ISBN 0-8027-8759-2 (Reinforced)
   1. Karelian bear dog—West (U.S.)—Juvenile literature. 2. Bears—Control—West
(U.S.)—Juvenile literature. [1. Karelian bear dog. 2. Dogs. 3. Bears—Control.] I. Title.
   SF429.K37 W66 2000
   636.73—dc21   00-043776

$16.95

Printed in Hong Kong

10 9 8 7 6 5 4 3 2 1

J
636.73
WOO
c.1

6-02

TOWNSHIP OF UNION
FREE PUBLIC LIBRARY